Jewish History in The United States

An overview of American Jewish history

Neil K. Taylor

Table of contents

Chapter 1

Judaism

The oldest monotheistic religion in the world is Judaism, which has been around for around 4,000 years. Jews believe that there is only one God, who revealed himself to them via the ancient prophets. Understanding Judaism's history is crucial since it has a long history of law, culture, and customs.

Faiths of Judaism
Jews hold the view that there is only one God, and this God has made a covenant, or unique arrangement, with them. Through prophets, their

God speaks to the faithful and praises good
actions while punishing the wicked.
With a few exceptions, the majority of Jews hold
the belief that their Messiah will one day arrive
but has not yet.

The spiritual leaders of Jews are known as
rabbis, and they worship in houses of worship
known as synagogues. The emblem of Judaism
is the six-pointed Star of David.
There are around 14 million Jews on the globe
today. They reside mostly in Israel and the
United States. According to custom, a person is
regarded as Jewish if his or her mother is Jewish.

Torah

The same books found in the Old Testament of the Christian Bible are found in the Jewish holy scripture known as the Tanakh, often known as the "Hebrew Bible," however they are arranged in a slightly different sequence.
The Torah, the first five books of the Tanakh, provides the rules that Jews must abide by. It is also sometimes known as the Pentateuch.

Inventor of Judaism

The Torah contains explanations of the Jewish faith's beginnings. The passage claims that Abraham, a Hebrew man who is regarded as the father of Judaism, was the one to whom God first showed himself.
Jews hold the view that Abraham and his offspring were chosen individuals who would establish a great country as a result of a particular covenant that God made with Abraham.

Both Isaac and Jacob, the grandson of Abraham, rose to prominence in early Jewish history. Jacob adopted the name Israel, and his offspring and subsequent generations came to be referred to as Israelites.

The Israelites were led out of Egypt by the prophet Moses after they had been held as slaves for hundreds of years, more than a thousand years after Abraham.

The Bible claims that God gave Moses the Ten Commandments—his set of laws—on Mount Sinai.

Temple's for Jews

The Jewish people were controlled by King David at about 1000 B.C. The first holy Temple was erected in Jerusalem by his son Solomon, who later made it the center of the Jewish religion.

Around 931 B.C., the Jewish people were divided into Israel in the north and Judah in the south when the monarchy broke apart.

The first Temple was demolished by the
Babylonians somewhere about 587 B.C., who
also exiled a large number of Jews.

The construction of a second Temple began
about 516 B.C. but was ultimately destroyed in
70 A.D. by the Romans.
Jewish people no longer had a central location to
congregate, so they turned their attention to
worshiping in nearby synagogues, which is why
the collapse of the second Temple was crucial.

Jewish Holy Scripture
Although the Tanakh (which contains the Torah)
is regarded as the holy book of Judaism,
numerous other significant manuscripts were
written in the following centuries. These
provided explanations on how the Tanakh should
be understood and recorded oral laws that had
not before been recorded.

The Jewish code of law, which was previously
transmitted orally, was described and explained

in the Mishnah, a work that was assembled by experts around the year 200 A.D.

Talmud
The Talmud, a compendium of teachings and commentary on Jewish law, was later produced. The Talmud comprises two texts: the Mishnah and the Gemara (which examines the Mishnah). It describes the significance of the 613 Jewish law commandments and incorporates the views of thousands of rabbis.
Around the third century A.D., the first Talmud manuscript was completed. In the fifth century A.D., the second form was finished.

Numerous more books and commentaries are included in Judaism. The 13 Articles of Faith, authored by the Jewish philosopher Maimonides, serve as one example.

Shabbat

For Jews, Shabbat is observed as a day of rest and prayer. Typically, it starts around dusk on Friday and lasts until dawn on Saturday. Depending on the kind of Judaism a Jewish family practices, observing Shabbat may take many different shapes. For instance, Orthodox and Conservative Jews may abstain from engaging in any physical work, utilizing any electrical equipment, or engaging in any other unlawful activity.

Persecution and Judaism

Jews have endured persecution for their religious convictions throughout history. A few well-known occasions are:

The Granada Massacre of 1066 occurred on December 30, when a Muslim mob seized control of the royal palace in Granada and massacred around 1,000 Jewish households.

Joseph ibn Naghrela, the Jewish vizier to the Berber ruler, was also abducted and executed by the gang.

The First Crusade: Thousands of Jews were slain, and many more were forced to convert to Christianity, during the first of the Crusades, a series of Christian and Muslim holy battles that took place in medieval times.

The Spanish Expulsion: In a royal order published in 1492, Spain's rulers commanded that any Jews who refused to convert to Christianity would be removed from the nation. According to experts, tens of thousands of people perished attempting to reach safety, and around 200,000 more were forced out.
The most notorious contemporary atrocity, the Holocaust, saw the Nazis slaughter more than 6 million Jews.
The Birth of Israel
Zionism, a movement for the establishment of a Jewish state that started in 19th-century Europe, was adopted by many Jews during and after the

Holocaust when they returned to their native country (in the Middle East area known as Palestine).

Israel gained its independence at a formal ceremony in 1948. The position of prime minister was bestowed to David Ben-Gurion, one of the foremost advocates of a Jewish nation-state.

For the Jewish people, who had arduously advocated for an independent state in their homeland, this event was seen as a success. But once Israel became a state, hostilities between Jews and Arabs in Palestine became worse and are still present today.

Type of Judaism

Judaism of the Orthodox: Orthodox Jews are distinguished by their stringent adherence to Jewish law and ritual. For instance, the majority agree that employment, transportation, and financial transactions should be avoided on Shabbat.

Hasidic Jews are one of the many subgroups within the variegated Orthodox Jewish movement. Contrary to orthodox or ultra-Orthodox Judaism, this kind of Judaism dates back to the 18th century in Eastern Europe. Hasidic Jews place a strong emphasis on a mystical encounter with God that entails close communication with him via prayer and worship. The Hasidic, Orthodox Jewish movement in Chabad is well-known.

Reform Judaism: Known as a liberal branch of the religion that places higher importance on ethical standards than exact fulfillment of Jewish law. People who follow encourage innovation and growth. Most Jews who reside in the United States adhere to Reform Judaism. to Reiner, "we'd have sent up someone like Mel Brooks instead of the astronauts if America truly wanted to comprehend space. If he had been allowed to get up there, can you imagine the questions we'd be asking about the universe?

Contemporary Moralists

In the Babylonian Talmud, God determines whether someone should be admitted to paradise by asking them four important questions. Did you handle your affairs honestly, to start?

Jewish tradition places a high priority on ethics, and centuries' worth of text and discussion is devoted to the problem of how to live a righteous life. It should come as no surprise that the ritual of asking and responding to these questions is thriving in America, although under mass-market guises, and Jews participate in the conversation.
Dr. Laura Schlessinger of Los Angeles, America's top radio talk show presenter, and two Jewish sisters from Iowa named Abigail Van Buren and Ann Landers also provide advice to millions of listeners.

These contemporary moralists cater to a general audience, yet their personal counsel has a strong Jewish element. Eppie Lederer's (Ann Landers) daughter Margo Howard said that her mother came from a household where kindness, common sense, and ceremonial Judaism were valued.

She said that being Jewish had influenced her emotional growth. "When the chance to answer letters at a newspaper presented itself, it was as if she had been doing it her whole life. She created a popularized version of Talmud, which is the idea that there is a fundamental moral code.

Both mundane everyday issues and life-and-death issues may be resolved through ethics. While millions of Jews reflect on the Holocaust in private, others have brought up the topics of responsibility and genocide in a more public setting.

The killing of 6 million Jews by Adolf Hitler sparked a heated controversy in the United States and internationally in 1978 because of NBC-"Holocaust." TV's When Steven

Spielberg's "Schindler's List" was shown 19 years later, the incident was repeated.

The Holocaust's message, according to award-winning author Gerald Green, extended well beyond the Jewish suffering and touched on a rising issue in multicultural America.

He said, "We must be extremely cautious not to allow our hatreds to grow out of control. "I believe we started a discussion. We started debating this matter so that others may discuss it.

David Gelber was inspired by the same need. He created two impactful films about Bosnia for ABC News in 1994. Veteran newsman Gelber said that his Jewish heritage had a major role in advocating for these programs.

He stated, "I watched as Bosnian Muslims were gathered up and massacred, and it reminded me of my own distant family who went through the same thing in Europe so many years earlier."

"How could it not hit home for a Jew in America? People claim that if the media had covered Auschwitz, the world would be quite different now. Bosnia was covered by the media, yet little changed.

Divergent perspectives on the future
Jews have made a significant and varied contribution to American culture. But the issue still remains: Will that presence diminish as integration goes on?

Since Israel is the only nation where Jews have enjoyed greater freedom than everywhere else, and anti-Semitism has been steadily declining, it is possible for people who were almost wiped out fifty years ago to feel optimistic about their future.

According to sociologist Seymor Martin Lipset, "logically, the integration of Jews into our society, the blurring of their ethnic characteristics, should lead to a reduction in the

quality of their contributions to American life."
"However, it hasn't so far. It will probably
survive.
What kind of survival, though?

Rabbi Wolpe warned that Jews would vanish if
they didn't make a strong new commitment to
their rituals and customs. "For what use is
survival for one's own sake? This is the
philosophy of the jungle, not the philosophy of a
people who ought to be holy.

Some people are even more negative. The
biggest Orthodox congregation on the West
Coast, Temple Beth Jacob in Beverly Hills, is
led by Rabbi Abner Weiss, who feels that Israel
is already taking over as the cultural leader of
the whole world's Jewry.

He replied, "I worry about this American
community. It won't be able to care for its
young, which is not promising.

Others struggle with the issue and come to a different conclusion: If Jews survived Hitler, they would undoubtedly survive MTV. Jews have thought about their annihilation for millennia.

Rabbi Angel remarked, "I believe too much energy is wasted worrying about the entire house of Israel. I think Judaism is on the ascent. Jews are rediscovering their Judaism throughout the nation. In 30 or 40 years, we may not be able to identify this community or its contributions, but it will still exist, she said. Our current task is to rekindle Jewish sentiment wherever we can.

In the end, it boils down to choosing an identity: Are Jews a unique ethnic group in our country, or should they essentially blend in with other Americans, as Woodrow Wilson said in the past? Professor Sachar said that the long-term cost of living in an ethnically homogenous ghetto or an open society for Jews in America would be too expensive.

The borders of Jewish life have really been eroding, he said. However, it is a little price to pay for the freedom we have experienced in this nation. An open, democratic society has too many benefits to ignore.

Conservative Judaism: This branch of Judaism is sometimes seen as falling between Orthodox and Reform Judaism. Conservative Jews often respect Jewish tradition while allowing for some modernization.

Reconstructionist Judaism: Mordecai Kaplan established the Society for the Advancement of Judaism in 1922, which is when reconstructionism first emerged. This group thinks that Judaism is a continuously developing religious civilization.
Rabbi Sherwin Wine established the humanistic branch of Judaism in 1963. Humanistic Jews honor Jewish tradition and history without placing a strong focus on God.

Judaism has several different denominations, although many Jews just refer to themselves as Jews without identifying with any specific category.

Jewish Festivals
Jewish people commemorate several significant historical dates and occasions, including:

Passover: This seven- or eight-day festival commemorates the liberation of the Jews from Egyptian slavery. Passover specifically relates to the biblical account of a plague that is claimed to have killed all other firstborn infants in Egypt, but the Hebrew God "passed over" the homes of Jewish families and preserved their children.

Rosh Hashanah: During this festival, sometimes referred to as the Jewish New Year, Jews commemorate the creation of the cosmos and mankind.

Yom Kippur: The Jewish people regard this "Day of Atonement" to be the holiest day of the

year, and they traditionally observe it by fasting
and prayer.
The High Holidays, also known as the Days of
Awe or Yamim Noraim, are the ten days that
begin with Rosh Hashanah and finish with Yom
Kippur. Jewish Jews see the High Holy Days as
a time of repentance.

Hanukkah: This eight-day Jewish holiday is
sometimes referred to as the "Festival of Lights."
Hanukkah commemorates the rededication of the
Jewish Temple in Jerusalem after the Maccabees'
victory over the Syrian Greeks more than two
thousand years ago.

The happy festival of Purim commemorates the
moment when the Jewish population of Persia
was spared from extinction.

Chapter 2

Jews in America: A Brief History

[1654]
**The first Jewish immigrants arrive in
America by sea.**

The roughly twenty-three Jews who fled Recife,
Brazil, and arrived in New Amsterdam in 1654
sought a permanent home—a place where they
could "travel," "trade," "live," and
"remain"—following the Portuguese recapture
of the Dutch colony, unlike earlier Jewish
travelers (such as Bohemian Jewish metallurgist
Joachim Gaunce, who was sent to Roanoke
Island in 1585 by Sir Walter Raleigh). Dr. Gary

Zola says that the year 1654 has taken on symbolic meaning. The Dutch West India Company's statement to the Dutch West India Company that the refugees are "a deceitful race, hateful enemies, and blasphemers of the name of Christ" is just one example of the hostility the refugees encountered right away. This dynamic is representative of the entire flow of American Jewish history. After a year, the Dutch West India Company, which was reliant on Jewish investors, gave the Jews of New Amsterdam permission to reside, under the condition that "the destitute among them shall...be sustained by their people."

[1730]
The first synagogue in North America, Congregation Shearith Israel, was constructed on Mill Street in New York City by fifty to sixty Jews of Spanish and Portuguese descent.

Congregation Shearith Israel provided Sephardic and Ashkenazic men and women with traditional services, religious instruction, kosher meat, and Passover supplies while serving as the sole synagogue in New York City up until 1825. Professor Deborah Dash Moore claims that "Even more than the arrival of Jews, the creation of this synagogue bespeaks a concern for the continuation of Jewish lives and communities."

[1787 & 1791]
In the years that followed the American Revolution, a conflict in which at least 100 American Jews are known to have taken part, the US Constitution and the Bill of Rights were adopted, providing Jews legal equality.

According to Professor Jonathan Sarna, "The Federal Constitution [1787] and the Bill of Rights [1791] barred Congress from passing any laws respecting an establishment of religion, or prohibiting the free exercise thereof...'." "Jews, therefore, acquired their religious freedom in the United States (and in most but not all of the different states), not as a result of a special privilege or "Jew bill" that marked them apart from everyone else, but rather as individuals. Jews had therefore attained an unheard-of level of "equal footing" in America by the end of the 18th century."

[1790]
The Hebrew Congregation in Newport, Rhode Island is where the first president of the United States delivered a cordial speech.

George Washington told the community that the US government "gives intolerance no sanction, to persecution no help" in a letter to the church, stating that freedom is "an inherent natural right." According to Rabbi David Ellenson, "George Washington's letter emphasized that America would be a country where Jews were accepted as equals and also reinforced the concept of tolerance as an American ideal."

[1824-1825]

Jewish reformers in Charleston, South Carolina ask Congregation Beth Elohim's leaders to make significant changes to the Sabbath service (a shorter service, English translations of Hebrew prayers, and a weekly sermon in English), and when their request is rejected, they found a new congregation that adheres to contemporary religious ideals.

The Sabbath Service and Miscellaneous Prayers Adopted by the Reformed Society of Israelites was the first Reform Jewish prayer book to be published in America. The Reformed Society of Israelites was determined to replace "blind observance of the ceremonial law" with "true piety," which they viewed as the "first great object of our Holy Religion." "For the first time, American Jews had a selection of churches to choose from, as opposed to only the conservative Sephardic congregations that had "established" themselves. Jews who didn't feel comfortable in synagogue also no longer had to give in to consensus to maintain their values; instead, they felt free to leave and formed their congregations. Congregational autonomy generally took hold in a free and democratic America, culminating in the emergence of a brand-new Judaism in America that is diverse and pluralistic."

[1838]
The first Hebrew Sunday school was established by Rebecca Gratz, the most well-known Jewish woman in America.

The daughter of a wealthy merchant, Gratz played a significant role in the establishment of Philadelphia's nondenominational Female Association for the Relief of Women and Children in Reduced Circumstances before focusing on education, where her efforts helped to found the Jewish Sunday school movement. Without it, Gary Zola asks, "Where would we be?" The majority of kids nowadays still attend Sunday school and other supplemental classes to learn about Judaism. Furthermore, according to Jonathan Sarna "By giving them responsibility for the religious instruction and spiritual direction of the children, Gratz's Sunday school changed the position of women in American Judaism. When Gratz passed away in 1869, the majority of American Jews who had any formal Jewish education at all had probably learned the majority of what they knew from female professors. These educators then needed to learn more about Judaism."

[1842]
A wave of Jewish immigration from Central Europe coincides with the founding of Har Sinai, the second congregation of Reform Judaism, in Baltimore.

A strong declaration of Jewishness in America was made by Har Sinai when it chose to follow the more conventional Baltimore Hebrew Congregation and install a six-pointed Magen David (Star of David) in its new structure's windows. Numerous other iconic synagogues would be built by German Jews during this decade, including B'nai Yeshurun (later known as Wise Temple) in Cincinnati (1842) and

Temple Emanu-El in New York City (1845).
According to Jonathan Sarna, "the young, urban,
upwardly mobile lay worshippers [at Emanu-El]
sought to recruit young people, arouse religious
fervor, and aid Jews in 'occupying a position of
higher respect' among their fellow citizens."
Other Reform churches imitated [Emanu- El's]
daring alterations to the worship service, which
included German songs, a sermon, a condensed
service, and organ music.

[1843]
To spread Judaism through peoplehood and
culture rather than through religion or belief,
twelve German Jewish immigrants to New
York's Lower East Side found B'nai B'rith (Sons
of the Covenant), the nation's first Jewish
fraternal society.

"According to Jonathan Sarna, in the past,
synagogues in each village had offered all the
services required by Jews, including caring for
the sick, helping widows and orphans, and

aiding out-of-town guests. However, there were now several synagogues in every town, and they were in direct competition with one another. The United Order of True Sisters, a sister organization of B'nai B'rith, asserted that 'unity and harmony could be achieved by fraternal connections, the covenant (b'rith) that united Jews regardless of their religious beliefs." As a consequence, an alternative to the synagogue was made available to American Jews for the first time.

[1845]
Isaac Leeser, the hazzan of Philadelphia's Congregation Mikveh Israel, founds the Jewish Publication Society, demonstrating the importance of the written word in keeping Judaism alive in the United States.

Gary Zola cites JPS as having "laid the scene for future Jewish publishing firms and literary works." The Jewish community would not have developed into a significant center for Jewish life without a place for fostering study, literature, and Jewish writing.e year 1654 has taken on symbolic meaning. The Dutch West India Company's statement to the Dutch West India Company that the refugees are "a deceitful race, hateful enemies, and blasphemers of the name of Christ" is just one example of the hostility the refugees encountered right away. This dynamic is representative of the entire flow of American Jewish history. After a year, the Dutch West India Company, which was reliant on Jewish investors, gave the Jews of New Amsterdam permission to reside, under the condition that "the destitute among them shall...be sustained by their own people."

[1730]
The first synagogue in North America, Congregation Shearith Israel, was constructed on Mill Street in New York City by fifty to sixty Jews of Spanish and Portuguese descent.

Congregation Shearith Israel provided Sephardic and Ashkenazic men and women with traditional services, religious instruction, kosher meat, and Passover supplies while serving as the sole synagogue in New York City up until 1825. Professor Deborah Dash Moore claims that, "Even more than the arrival of Jews, the creation of this synagogue bespeaks a concern for the continuation of Jewish lives and communities."

[1787 & 1791]
In the years that followed the American Revolution, a conflict in which at least 100 American Jews are known to have taken part, the US Constitution and the Bill of Rights were adopted, providing Jews legal equality.

According to Professor Jonathan Sarna, "The Federal Constitution [1787] and the Bill of Rights [1791] barred Congress from passing any laws'respecting an establishment of religion, or prohibiting the free exercise thereof...'." "Jews therefore acquired their religious freedom in the United States (and in most but not all of the different states), not as a result of a special privilege or "Jew bill" that marked them apart from everyone else, but rather as individuals. Jews had therefore attained an unheard-of level of "equal footing" in America by the end of the 18th century."

[1790]
The Hebrew Congregation in Newport, Rhode Island is where the first president of the United States delivered a cordial speech.

George Washington told the community that the US government "gives to intolerance no sanction, to persecution no help" in a letter to the church, stating that freedom is "an inherent natural right." According to Rabbi David Ellenson, "George Washington's letter emphasized that America would be a country where Jews were accepted as equals and also reinforced the concept of tolerance as an American ideal."

[1824-1825]

Jewish reformers in Charleston, South Carolina ask Congregation Beth Elohim's leaders to make significant changes to the Sabbath service (a shorter service, English translations of Hebrew prayers, and a weekly sermon in English), and when their request is rejected, they found a new congregation that adheres to contemporary religious ideals.

The Sabbath Service and Miscellaneous Prayers Adopted by the Reformed Society of Israelites was the first Reform Jewish prayer book to be published in America. The Reformed Society of Israelites was determined to replace "blind observance of the ceremonial law" with "true piety," which they viewed as the "first great object of our Holy Religion." "For the first time, American Jews had a selection of churches to choose from, as opposed to only the conservative Sephardic congregations that had "established" themselves. Jews who didn't feel comfortable in synagogue also no longer had to give in to consensus in order to maintain their values; instead, they felt free to leave and formed their own congregations. Congregational autonomy generally took hold in a free and democratic America, culminating in the emergence of a brand-new Judaism in America that is diverse and pluralistic."

[1838]
First Hebrew Sunday school established by Rebecca Gratz, the most well-known Jewish woman in America.

The daughter of a wealthy merchant, Gratz played a significant role in the establishment of Philadelphia's nondenominational Female Association for the Relief of Women and Children in Reduced Circumstances before focusing on education, where her efforts helped to found the Jewish Sunday-school movement. Without it, Gary Zola asks, "Where would we be?" The majority of kids nowadays still attend Sunday school and other supplemental classes to learn about Judaism. Furthermore, according to Jonathan Sarna "By giving them responsibility for the religious instruction and spiritual direction of the children, Gratz's Sunday school changed the position of women in American Judaism. When Gratz passed away in 1869, the majority of American Jews who had any formal Jewish education at all had probably learnt the majority of what they knew from female professors. These educators then needed to learn more about Judaism.

[1842]
A wave of Jewish immigration from Central Europe coincides with the founding of Har Sinai, the second congregation of Reform Judaism, in Baltimore.

A strong declaration of Jewishness in America was made by Har Sinai when it chose to follow the more conventional Baltimore Hebrew Congregation and install a six-pointed Magen David (Star of David) in its new structure's windows. Numerous other iconic synagogues would be built by German Jews during this decade, including B'nai Yeshurun (later known

as Wise Temple) in Cincinnati (1842) and
Temple Emanu-El in New York City (1845).
According to Jonathan Sarna, "the young, urban,
upwardly mobile lay worshippers [at Emanu-El]
sought to recruit young people, arouse religious
fervor, and aid Jews in 'occupying a position of
higher respect' among their fellow citizens."
Other Reform churches imitated [Emanu- El's]
daring alterations to the worship service, which
included German songs, a sermon, a condensed
service, and organ music.

[1843]
In order to spread Judaism through peoplehood and culture rather than through religion or belief, twelve German Jewish immigrants to New York's Lower East Side found B'nai B'rith (Sons of the Covenant), the nation's first Jewish fraternal society.

"According to Jonathan Sarna, in the past, synagogues in each village had offered all the services required by Jews, including caring for the sick, helping widows and orphans, and aiding out-of-town guests. However, there were now several synagogues in every town, and they were in direct competition with one another. The United Order of True Sisters, a sister organization of B'nai B'rith, asserted that 'unity and harmony' could be achieved by fraternal connections, the covenant (b'rith) that united Jews regardless of their religious beliefs." As a consequence, an alternative to the synagogue

was made available to American Jews for the
first time.

[1845]
**Isaac Leeser, the hazzan of Philadelphia's
Congregation Mikveh Israel, founds the
Jewish Publication Society, demonstrating the
importance of the written word in keeping
Judaism alive in the United States.**

Gary Zola cites JPS as having "laid the scene for
future Jewish publishing firms and literary
works." The Jewish
community would not have developed into a
significant center for Jewish life without a place
for fostering study, literature, and Jewish
writing.

[1859]
The Board of Delegates of American Israelites
was established to "keep a watchful eye on all
occurrences at home and abroad" by twenty-four
primarily Ashkenazic congregations in response

to a perceived lack of American Jewish unity in the face of political unrest. The congregations were commanded by Shaaray Tefilla of New York and Isaac Leeser of Philadelphia.

A year before, it was found that Italian 6-year-old Edgardo Mortara had been surreptitiously baptized by his nursemaid. As a result, his house was raided, and he was given over to the Catholic Church. In Italy, it was illegal for anybody, even a Catholic's own parents, to raise a Jewish child. James Buchanan, president of the United States, declined to become involved despite multiple requests from different American Jewish organizations, saying that the US shouldn't interfere in the affairs of other sovereign states. Jewish leaders created a Board of Delegates, patterning it after the prominent Jewish Board of Deputies in London, believing that their own disarray was the reason their plea had failed. However, owing to inter-communal strife, only a tiny portion of the synagogues in America participated. Nevertheless, according to Gary Zola, "the

Board's establishment reflected the early commitment of American Jewry to utilize their political power at home to support besieged Jews everywhere."

[1862]
After Major General Ulysses S. Grant orders the deportation of Jews from his combat zone due to suspected smuggling and cotton speculation and threatens any who might return with arrest and detention, Jews take their cause to the White House.

President Abraham Lincoln gave Army General Henry Halleck the authority to reverse Grant's order after meetings with Cincinnati Congressman John A. Gurley and Paducah, Kentucky, Jew Cesar Kaskel. President Lincoln later addressed a gathering of Jewish leaders and said: "To say anything negative about a class is to mix the good with the evil. I dislike hearing a group of people, whether it is from a class or a country, be vilified because of a few sinners." According to Pamela Nadell, this was a striking example of Jewish confidence. The President of the United States was now reachable by Jews. Jonathan Sarna continues, "This experience strengthened Jews with the knowledge that they could fight back against discrimination and prevail—even against a well-known general."

[1873]

Rabbi Isaac Mayer Wise, a German immigrant, established the Central Conference of American Rabbis and the Union of American Hebrew Congregations before founding Cincinnati's Hebrew Union College, the nation's first functional rabbinical seminary, and the Union of American Hebrew Congregations in 1875. (1889).

According to Jonathan Sarna, Rabbi Wise traversed the whole nation while lecturing, establishing new synagogues, and evangelizing for Jewish religious reform. However, he was successful in developing, institutionalizing, and directing American Reform Judaism. In the end, his attempt to unite all American Jews failed.

Rabbi Wise's plan, which included a synagogue
umbrella organization, rabbinic school, and
rabbinic association, was eventually replicated
by other American Jewish denominational
groups. This model would go on to influence the
framework of organized Jewish religious life in
America. Deborah Dash Moore says that the first
indigenous Jewish leadership in America was
trained as a result of the establishment of those
Jewish academies. Jews were starting to create
what may be termed an American Judaism as
they became more aware that America required
specific characteristics that were alien to the
European experience. As a result, they stopped
selecting leaders from Europe.

[1881]
Beginning in Eastern Europe, a large-scale Jewish exodus will change American Jewry.

Pogroms that swept through Russia following
the death of Tsar Alexander II sparked an
epochal migration that would bring two million
Eastern European Jews to America, whose

cultural and religious traditions were very different from those of the Central European Jews who were already comfortably settled in the country. According to Jonathan Sarna, these immigrants' religious requirements altered as a result of their Americanization. "They desired a more "refined" worship experience, more in line with their growing social position, just like the Central European Jews had done before them. [They] made a dramatic entry into the American religious arena in an effort to achieve religious equality. Their magnificent synagogues and cantors highlighted their Americanization, their increased self-confidence, and their ascending social status."

[1912]
Hadassah, founded by Henrietta Szold, eventually grows to become the biggest women's organization in the US as well as the largest American Zionist organization.

Henrietta Szold, who was the spiritual head of Baltimore's Congregation Oheb Shalom and the daughter of Rabbi Benjamin Szold, would be a significant figure in the politicking of American Jewish women. The Hadassah Chapter of Daughters of Zion was founded on February 24, 1912, by 38 women. Szold was chosen as the organization's first president two years later at their inaugural convention. Deborah Dash Moore quotes Hadassah as saying that they "recruited numerous generations of American Jewish women to political and social action on behalf of the Yishuv and Israel."

[1916]
The first Jewish Supreme Court judge is American Zionist leader Louis Brandeis.

"Brandeis' appointment," according to Gary Zola, "marked a pivotal moment for American Jews, who took deep pride in the achievements of one of their own and saw that Jews could rise to the highest levels of American society." Pamela Nadell continues, "It was obvious that a

Jew who identified with Jewish concerns could reach the highest echelons of government and serve the American people and our country.

[1934]
Judaism as a Civilization: Toward a Reconstruction of American-Jewish Life, written by Lithuanian-born professor Mordecai M. Kaplan of the Jewish Theological Seminary, is one of the most significant Jewish works of the 20th century.

articulating a new understanding of Judaism that paved the way for the emergence of a new movement known as Reconstructionist Judaism.

Judaism, according to Jonathan Sarna, embraces "every Jew and everything Jewish, including land (meaning Israel), history, language, literature, religious folkways, mores, laws, and art." Kaplan taught that Judaism is more than just a religion. It is also a vibrant religious civilization. Across the board in American Jewish religious life, he claims, two of Kaplan's

concepts have gained widespread acceptance.
First, "As a result of Kaplan's emphasis on the
"whole life of the Jew," previously undervalued
facets of Jewish culture like the arts, crafts,
music, drama, dance, and food began to receive
more attention. Over time, cultural programs
started to permeate Jewish communities and
almost every synagogue. Second, he set the stage
for the development of the synagogue-center
movement by advocating for a synagogue-center
that would transform the place of worship
into a multipurpose hub of Jewish communal life
open seven days a week."

[1943]
After their convoy ship is destroyed by the
Germans, four chaplains—a Catholic priest
(John P. Washington), a Dutch Reform minister
(Clark V. Poling), a Methodist reverend (George
L. Fox), and a Reform rabbi (Alexander D.
Goode)—die at sea as heroes.

As the Dorchester fell under the waters, the
chaplains gave up their life jackets and stood

arm in arm, praying for the soldiers, encouraging them to have bravery in the face of disaster. According to Deborah Dash Moore, "their coordinated action was a tremendous symbolic moment, communicating to the whole public the unifying ideals that Jews, Protestants, and Catholics all share."

[1945]
A half million Jewish GIs' time in the US military during World War II changed them on a generational level.

According to Deborah Dash Moore, in many respects, this experience marked the "coming of age" of American Jews. "Jewish troops left the war more American and more Jewish than they had entered. They had learned to push back when provoked, and as a result, they were no longer prepared to accept second-class citizenship. Instead, they were prepared to fight for a Jewish state and for their rights as Jews to be protected from discrimination. They also realized that the US accepted Judaism as a part of the Judeo-Christian tradition. Finally, as they got to know people from other parts of the country, they realized they could settle and integrate outside of the confines of their childhood homes."

[1947]
In a UN resolution calling for the division of Palestine into two states—one Jewish and one Arab—the United States joined 32 other countries.

One year later, the State of Israel formally proclaims its independence. Jenna Weissman Joselit claims that Jews all throughout the globe experienced "pride and comfort." "Everything had been so hopeless before Israel was born; this was a tremendous time of promise," said the author. According to Jonathan Sarna, "Zionists offered American Jews (as well as other Diaspora groups) a feeling of duty and an aim to unify behind.

[1948]

**In Waltham, Massachusetts, a group of
Jewish community leaders founds Brandeis,
the nation's first Jewishly financed
nonreligious university.**

While some of the school's early supporters
thought Brandeis would provide the best Jewish
minds in America with access to excellent higher
education (who might otherwise be denied due
to admissions quotas), Brandeis' first president,
Abram L. Sachar, saw the university as "a
corporate gift of Jews to higher education." In
fact, according to Gary Zola, "Jews and
non-Jews from all over the globe study together
in a premier academic institution that is
associated with the highest intellectual goals of
American Jewry."

**[1955]
In his best-selling book
Protestant-Catholic-Jew, Will Herberg claims
that these three religiously oriented societies
make up America, calling it a "triple melting
pot."**

Jonathan Sarna notes that despite making up just 3.2% of the country's population, Jews were "enfranchised as the custodians of one-third of the American religious history" as a result of Herberg. Herberg's thesis "caught the imagination and molded future religious debate in America" despite its obvious flaws.

[1963]
Jews are important participants in the Washington, DC, civil rights march.

The president of the American Jewish Congress and co-organizer of the march, Rabbi Joachim Prinz, who served as the rabbi of the Berlin Jewish community under the Nazi regime, addressed the crowd just before Martin Luther King Jr. gave his renowned "I Have a Dream" speech. Instead of advocating for quiet change, he urged fervent Jewish communal action. According to Jonathan Sarna, "for Prinz and those who followed in his footsteps, the Holocaust served as a Jewish reference point, providing a specifically Jewish justification for involvement in the civil rights movement, as well as a universal reference point that underscored the moral righteousness of antiracist activism." Many Jewish leaders and activists, including UAHC President Rabbi Maurice Eisendrath, Rabbi Abraham Joshua Heschel, and others, would travel to the South to protest racial injustice; in 1964, President Lyndon Johnson signed into law the Civil Rights Act and the Voting Rights Act, both of which had been written at the Religious Action Center of Reform Judaism.

[1965]
Because the first game of the Dodgers-Minnesota World Series occurs on Yom Kippur, Sandy Koufax declines to take the mound.

According to David Ellenson, "Koufax's reluctance to pitch gave American Jews a great feeling of pride in their Jewishness." "One of the

greatest baseball players in American history
was standing up and announcing to the public
his Jewish identity and practices. Jews have
always taken great satisfaction in their reputation
as independent, devoted to their religion, and
willing to stand up for their moral principles."

[1967]
**American Jews contribute $430 million to
Israel despite worries of a second Holocaust
and threats from Arab countries to push the
Jewish state into the sea.**

Israeli victory is crucial in the Six-Day War.
According to Jonathan Sarna, "Israel's triumph
signified more than Superman-like heroics for
many American Jews." It was largely believed to
be an American win. David Ellenson adds: "Two
decades after the Holocaust, this unexpected and
almost miraculous win caused a collective sigh
of relief among American Jews, who also felt an
almost limitless sense of pride. Jew was no
longer a helpless victim."

[1972]
**The first American woman to be ordained a
rabbi is Sally Jane Priesand, a graduate of the
Hebrew Union College-Jewish Institute of
Religion.**

Amy Eisenberg became the first woman
Conservative rabbi in 1985, while Sandy
Eisenberg became the first woman
Reconstructionist rabbi two years later.
According to Jenna Weissman Joselit,
"welcoming women into the rabbinate
transformed the rabbinate and demonstrated that
women were as competent as males." The
language of prayers altered as a result, with God
no longer being referred to as the Lord and many
references to the matriarchs, among other
changes to Jewish life in America.

/1993]
**In Washington, DC, the United States
Holocaust Memorial Museum is situated close
to the National Mall.**

The US government museum was founded to preserve the memory of the Shoah and was granted authorization by a unanimous Act of Congress. Since its establishment, it has educated over two million people annually about the history of the Holocaust and the dangers of bigotry. According to Gary Zola, "the Holocaust museum connects a Jewish tale with a human story and an American one." And it relates to the unanswered issue that lingers in the minds of a lot of American Jews: Did Americans—Jews and non-Jews—do enough as the tragedy unfolded?

[2000]
Senator Joseph Lieberman of Connecticut is the first Jew to get a major political party's nomination for vice president of the United States.

According to Jonathan Sarna, "Lieberman's enthusiastic reception by the American people transmitted the message that a Jew need not forsake his or her religion or religious traditions in order to aspire to high political office." The Al Gore/Joseph Lieberman ticket, says David Ellenson, "showed how well-entrenched and at-home Jews are in the United States."

[2004]
The Library of Congress, the National Archives and Records Administration, the American Jewish Historical Society, and the Jacob Rader Marcus Center of the American Jewish Archives collaborated to create the Commission for Commemorating 350 Years of American Jewish History. Congress also adopted a resolution honoring and recognizing the 350th anniversary of Jewish communal life in North America.

"This historic cooperation represents the first time in our nation's history that such a collaboration [of governmental and Jewish organizations] has taken place in a shared endeavor to deepen our knowledge of the American Jewish experience," claims Gary Zola.

The history of American Jews is, in a way, "coming of age" with this event.

This timeline was created after discussions with six eminent Jewish American academics: Dr. Gary Zola, an associate professor of the American Jewish Experience at Hebrew Union College-Jewish Institute of Religion in Cincinnati, and the executive director of the Jacob Rader Marcus Center of the American Jewish Archives; Professor Pamela Nadell, an authority on women's history at American University; Rabbi David Ellenson, a professor of Jewish religious thought and the president of HUC-JIR.

Chapter 3

Contributing to American Culture

THE NEW YORK "In America, they are not
Jews. They are citizens of the USA.
Wilson Woodrow

American Jews are uncomfortable posing, much
alone responding to, a crucial question for a
group that has historically been rife with
disagreement, dissent, and Talmudic disputes:
What impact have Jews had on American
culture? What uniquely Jewish contributions
have they made to our national culture?
According to Rabbi Alfred Wolf, founding head
of the Skirball Institute on American Values and
rabbi emeritus of Los Angeles' Wilshire
Boulevard Temple, "We've spent years exploring

how America has touched Jewish people, how it's transformed us." But when you ask the opposite question, you don't get much of a response.

The simple temptation is to provide a long list of Jews and their accomplishments, including Hall of Famers who are heavily weighted with Nobel Prize winners, playwrights, musicians, and artists, as well as a parade of businessmen, movie moguls, educators, journalists, and entertainers who have had an impact on American culture.
Indeed, Jewish leaders influenced the labor and civil rights movements, two of the country's biggest battles. The postwar American novel was essentially created by authors like Norman Mailer, Bernard Malamud, Saul Bellow, and Philip Roth.

The roster includes Bernstein, Spielberg, Streisand, Gershwin, and more. There is, however, a dearth of writing on Judaism and American culture in the search for a more profound response to the query—a theory that would account for the contributions of figures as disparate as Jerry Seinfeld and Albert Einstein.

Jews are having intense internal disagreements over their assimilation into American culture and how this is eroding their sense of self as they look to the future. Many are arguing about intermarriage and how it may significantly lower the number of Jews in the future.
These disputes go beyond personal disputes. Will Jews' significant contributions to our national life fade along with their identity if they are actually in danger due to their success here?

According to Rabbi David Wolpe of Sinai Temple, the oldest Conservative Jewish community in Los Angeles, "the farther you go from the root of your tradition, the less of a contribution you could be expected to make in a nation like America." "We could lose something important."

So what has the Jewish community in America specifically contributed?

The Torah could have the solution. Like all religions, Judaism is best understood via its holy tales, and the first five books of the Bible are rife with them.

One is Passover, which emphasizes human rights. Another example is God's Ten Commandments, which combine morality with law. The tale of Jacob's struggle with the angel, however, may reveal the most about Jews and their distinctive contributions.

Tradition has it that Jacob had been exiled in the wilderness for 20 years. He engaged in a furious struggle with a guy till dawn one night while by himself at the banks of a river. When the stranger saw that Jacob would not give in, he tore his hip out of its socket, leaving Jacob with a limp for the rest of his life.

Jacob was given the new name Israel, which means "one who wrestles with God," by the man

before he left. According to the legend, all of his
offspring will thereafter go by the same name.
Biblical historians have argued over the specifics
for ages, such as whether Jacob wrestled with
God or an angel or a human being. He was
battling with himself, wasn't he, whether he was
really alone? And what does the uncomfortable
limp he has always had to mean?

The underlying message is that Jews have
always engaged in spiritual conflict, according to
Wolf. "They provide challenging queries. They
disagree with conventional knowledge. They are
dubious.

He said, "Jews have traditionally been outsiders
because they are a minority, and the limp of
Jacob is what really distinguishes them. It serves
as a sign of uniqueness.
God's opponents. Iconoclasts. Subversives.
Pioneers.
Jews have always relied on cunning to get by.
Wolpe noticed that they have never fully

assimilated the ideals of those who dislike them,
unlike other oppressed groups. Education has
traditionally been respected there, and the
concept of intellectual independence is stressed.

Jews of all stripes, from the most ardently pious
to those who are disaffiliated from the religion,
are colored by this strong blend.
Rabbi Camille Angel of Congregation Rodeph
Sholom in New York said, "I have Jewish
friends who are leftists, social activists, and they
do not follow their faith. But if you ask them
why they get engaged, they'll say that it's
because they are aware of and recall that we
were all Pharaoh's slaves.

"You were outsiders in the Egyptian country."
The expression is a cornerstone of Jewish
identity and appears 36 times in the Torah.

How can Jews overlook the less fortunate people
living among them if they are aware of the fact
that they were once slaves, too? Nevertheless,
despite their comfort in a country like America,
Jews nevertheless retain painful memories of
oppression, from the Pharaoh to Hitler.
Thomas Cahill, the author of "The Gifts of the
Jews," once stated, "Individuals at the periphery
usually perceive more than people at the center."

According to Rabbi Arthur Hertzberg, a
historian, philosopher, and Talmudic scholar
who has written extensively on the history of
Judaism, American Jews have experienced
unique communal anguish from colonial times.

He said, "This Jewish anger is the wellspring of
Nobel awards and it's what drives Sammy."
Political dissent is one of its many guises, and it
also fuels a significant artistic contribution. It's
also a talent for conversation and a propensity
for posing serious ethical questions about the .
society we live in.

Jews struggle with politics, culture, and ethics, but not always honorably. American celebrities like David Begelman, Michael Milken, and Ivan Boesky were held accountable for their crimes. Amoral artists like Woody Allen have caused sorrow and controversy due to things that have happened in their personal lives.

Rabbi Wolf said, "A Jew is not a Jew just because he has fought an angel. But overall, we have contributed much to the history of our country.

A Political Tradition of Liberals

From a political perspective, that position has been quite unusual. Jews are the only prosperous ethnic group in America that does not often vote with their wallet, as many observers have noted. American Jews have often supported left-leaning candidates and issues, dating back to the first significant wave of immigration in the middle of the 19th century. As Jews supported FDR and the New Deal, that liberal slant expanded even more.

Jews are now among the wealthiest people in society, yet they have not given up their liberalism and migrated to the right. According to a recent Times survey of American Jews, 28% of Jews identify as moderates, 28% as conservatives and 46% Jews identify as liberals. According to author and history professor Howard Sachar of George Washington University, Jews are attentive to the political milieu wherever they go and are open to progressive ideas because of their past. This has been a political-based allegiance rather than a religious one.

It's a tough pill for Jews on the political right to swallow. Jewish liberal beliefs, according to Norman Podhoretz, a former editor of Commentary and one of the movement's founders, are based on political ignorance and sentimentality.

He said, "There's something unreasonable about
it. This is what people used to say about the
generals who fought in the previous conflict.
Jews remember Hitler and left-leaning European
parties that were friendlier than the right.
Today, evangelical Christians like Pat Robertson
and others are truly close allies of Israel.
Nevertheless, many Jews on the political left
have a deep-seated dread of them.
many liberals respond with a good cause.

Whatever kind of Jew you are, becoming
engaged will happen if you look in the mirror
every year and declare, "I am a member of a
band of former slaves," according to Rabbi
Arthur Waskow, a pioneer of the Jewish
Renewal Movement.

There are many examples: Reform One of the
few branches of any organized religion in our
nation that accepts and accommodates LGBT
worshipers is Judaism. Jews have been at the

forefront of many social concerns, including
feminism and the environment.

Regarding the civil rights movement, it is
difficult to envision it without the contributions
of Jews, at least from the 1940s through the
1970s. Despite the tense state of black and
Jewish relations today, their shared history is
remarkable.

Synagogues all throughout America contributed
money and personnel to the cause; Jewish
leaders planned some of the biggest rallies, and
two of the three civil rights activists who were
killed in Mississippi in 1964 were Jews.

According to Cahill, "Jews contributed strength
to that movement, and the muscle was a
yearning for justice."

The fact that Jews have been a people rooted in
the study of religious texts and commentary on
them for generations also explains one of the
faster Jewish assimilations into American

culture. America has a comparable intellectual concentration with its Constitution and layers of judicial judgment.

According to author Cynthia Ozick, "It's no coincidence that many American Jews have been drawn to constitutional law." The American judicial system and Jews are a great match, so it's always a text and dispute with us.

Jewish traditions and the development of social welfare programs fit together similarly well, despite the fact that Jews on the political left and right have strong opinions about why this is the case.

The welfare state, according to Hertzberg, "has a helluva lot more to do with the Jew than almost anyone else." "This is where the notion that unemployed people simply cannot be on the streets came from. It dates back a very long time.

Hogwash," Podhoretz remarked.

When you attribute any of this to the Jewish religion, you must exercise extreme caution, he advised. "A Jew today is more likely to be conservative the more religious he is. Therefore, it is difficult to claim that Judaism somehow fosters liberal attitudes.

In reference to the renowned Jewish scholar from the 12th century, "I mean, Maimonides had no comment on the balanced budget debate," Podhoretz said. We can't really argue that he would have been against HMOs even though he was a doctor. It's not just a Jewish problem.

But the dispute is a Jewish one fueled by antiquated texts, ferocious political wrangling, and contemporary issues.

Between the Lines: Jewish Stories
Jews were given a place to call intellectual homes in America, but they were also free to relocate. if they wanted, could reside in a more upscale section of the city. Jewish cultural contributions to American culture are dominated

by the idea of a restless movement from the
ancient to the new.

Take "The Jazz Singer," a 1927 movie where Al
Jolson became the first actor to ever speak in a
movie. It was a sharp depiction of the problems
confronting Eastern European Jews who were
leaving behind the stuffy ghettos of their
American boyhood, and it was wildly popular
with mainstream audiences.

"Kol Nidre," perhaps the holiest chant in the
religion, could only be on the same show as
"Toot, Toot, Tootsie, Goodbye" in a Jewish tale
of transformation and progress. And the
conclusion, in which Jolson pays tribute to his
ailing, patriarchal father before starting a show
business career, was poignant.

According to Rabbi Wolpe, "Hollywood
conveyed Jewish tales behind the scenes." The
underlying failing of Hollywood and Jewish
ingenuity in America is that it hasn't been Jewish

enough, yet those who founded the studios are subject to criticism.

Undoubtedly, the forerunners of silent and talking movies created parables about the importance of social fairness, underdog esteem, devotion, and family values. Neal Gabler, a historian, demonstrated how many Jewish producers and moguls were only reproducing the tales of their childhoods in Eastern Europe on the big screen in his book "An Empire of Their Own."

However, Wolpe noted that the fundamental Jewish ideals of instruction, morality, and tradition were missing. The people who constructed the studios often denied or felt ashamed of their own Jewishness.

In "Portnoy's Complaint" and other works by Philip Roth, Jews experience a similar rite of passage where they are torn between maintaining their ethnic identity and hastening to integrate. The same can be said for significant works by playwright Arthur Miller and musician George Gershwin, according to Hertzberg.

He said that although the main character of "Porgy and Bess" tries to get away from Catfish Row, the real tale "mirrors Gershwin's own rise from the Lower East Side to the top of Manhattan society. To become an American hero, he left behind an immigrant slum.

Hertzberg said that Miller's "Death of a Salesman" is really a sanitized Yiddish drama from New York's 2nd Avenue that portrays traditional Jewish conflicts.

You won't get along with the Goyim until they like you, Willy Loman tells his son. But already, the youngster is too American. Why should I kiss their ass, he queries? The play is one that is equally understandable in Yiddish and English.

Jews who immigrate to America repeatedly find new creative forms, and the outcomes may be spectacular. Examples include Bob Dylan integrating folk music and rock; Leonard Bernstein blending jazz and opera; and Alan Ginsburg launching the Beat poetry movement.

America has also been influenced by Jewish humor. Jewish humor has ridiculed human flaws and made millions of people laugh at themselves, from borscht belt stand-ups to the kings of TV comedy, Jack Benny, Milton Berle, and George Burns.

According to actor and director Rob Reiner, "One huge reason is that so much of our comedy comes from a place of grief." "Jews have endured everything, from Egypt through the pogroms and the Holocaust, so it strikes a deep emotional core.

You may connect to this way of seeing the world, he said, even if you're not Jewish.

According to Reiner, "we'd have sent up someone like Mel Brooks instead of the astronauts if America truly wanted to comprehend space. If he had been allowed to get up there, can you imagine the questions we'd be asking about the universe?

Contemporary Moralists

In the Babylonian Talmud, God determines whether someone should be admitted to paradise by asking them four important questions. Did you handle your affairs honestly, to start?

Jewish tradition places a high priority on ethics, and centuries' worth of text and discussion is devoted to the problem of how to live a righteous life. It should come as no surprise that the ritual of asking and responding to these questions is thriving in America, although under mass-market guises, and Jews participate in the conversation.

Dr. Laura Schlessinger of Los Angeles, America's top radio talk show presenter, and two Jewish sisters from Iowa named Abigail Van

Buren and Ann Landers also provide advice to millions of listeners.

These contemporary moralists cater to a general audience, yet their personal counsel has a strong Jewish element. Eppie Lederer's (Ann Landers) daughter Margo Howard said that her mother came from a household where kindness, common sense, and ceremonial Judaism were valued.

She said that being Jewish had influenced her emotional growth. "When the chance to answer letters at a newspaper presented itself, it was as if she had been doing it her whole life. She created a popularized version of Talmud, which is the idea that there is a fundamental moral code.

Both mundane everyday issues and life-and-death issues may be resolved through ethics. While millions of Jews reflect on the Holocaust in private, others have brought up the topics of responsibility and genocide in a more public setting.

The killing of 6 million Jews by Adolf Hitler sparked a heated controversy in the United States and internationally in 1978 because of NBC-"Holocaust." TV's When Steven Spielberg's "Schindler's List" was shown 19 years later, the incident was repeated.

The Holocaust's message, according to award-winning author Gerald Green, extended well beyond the Jewish suffering and touched on a rising issue in multicultural America.

He said, "We must be extremely cautious not to allow our hatreds to grow out of control. "I believe we started a discussion. We started debating this matter so that others may discuss it.

David Gelber was inspired by the same need. He created two impactful films about Bosnia for ABC News in 1994. Veteran newsman Gelber said that his Jewish heritage had a major role in advocating for these programs.

He stated, "I watched as Bosnian Muslims were gathered up and massacred, and it reminded me of my own distant family who went through the same thing in Europe so many years earlier."

"How could it not hit home for a Jew in America? People claim that if the media had covered Auschwitz, the world would be quite different now. Bosnia was covered by the media, yet little changed.

Divergent perspectives on the future

Jews have made a significant and varied contribution to American culture. But the issue still remains: Will that presence diminish as integration goes on?

Since Israel is the only nation where Jews have enjoyed greater freedom than everywhere else, and anti-Semitism has been steadily declining, it

is possible for people who were almost wiped
out fifty years ago to feel optimistic about their
future.

According to sociologist Seymor Martin Lipset,
"logically, the integration of Jews into our
society, the blurring of their ethnic
characteristics, should lead to a reduction in the
quality of their contributions to American life."
"However, it hasn't so far. It will probably
survive.

What kind of survival, though?

Rabbi Wolpe warned that Jews would vanish if
they didn't make a strong new commitment to
their rituals and customs. "For what use is
survival for one's own sake? This is the
philosophy of the jungle, not the philosophy of a
people who ought to be holy.

Some people are even more negative. The
biggest Orthodox congregation on the West
Coast, Temple Beth Jacob in Beverly Hills, is

led by Rabbi Abner Weiss, who feels that Israel is already taking over as the cultural leader of the whole world's Jewry.

He replied, "I worry about this American community. It won't be able to care for its young, which is not promising.

Others struggle with the issue and come to a different conclusion: If Jews survived Hitler, they would undoubtedly survive MTV. Jews have thought about their annihilation for millennia.

Rabbi Angel remarked, "I believe too much energy is wasted worrying about the entire house of Israel. I think Judaism is on the ascent.

Jews are rediscovering their Judaism throughout the nation. In 30 or 40 years, we may not be able to identify this community or its contributions, but it will still exist, she said. Our current task is to rekindle Jewish sentiment wherever we can.

In the end, it boils down to choosing an identity:
Are Jews a unique ethnic group in our country,
or should they essentially blend in with other
Americans, as Woodrow Wilson said in the past?

Professor Sachar said that the long-term cost of
living in an ethnically homogenous ghetto or an
open society for Jews in America would be too
expensive.

The borders of Jewish life have really been
eroding, he said. However, it is a little price to
pay for the freedom we have experienced in this
nation. An open, democratic society has too
many benefits to ignore.